The Essential Margaret Avison

The Essential
Margaret Avison

selected by Robyn Sarah

The Porcupine's Quill

Library and Archives Canada Cataloguing in Publication

Avison, Margaret, 1918–2007
[Poems. Selections]
b 35560551
    The essential Margaret Avison / selected by Robyn Sarah. – First.

(Essential poets; 6)
Poems.
ISBN 978-0-88984-333-2

    I. Sarah, Robyn, 1949– II. Title. III. Title: Poems. Selections.
IV. Series: Essential poets; 6

PS8501.V5A6 2010   C811'.54   C2010-903544-5

The following selections are © The Estate of Margaret Avison and are
reprinted here with the kind permission of McClelland & Stewart.
'Finished When Unfinished', 'Prayer of Anticipation', 'En Route', 'Poetry Is'
(from *Momentary Dark*, M&S, 2006); 'Still Life', 'Metamorphosis', 'Safe but
Shaky' (from *Listening*, M&S, 2009).

Published by The Porcupine's Quill, 68 Main Street, PO Box 160,
Erin, Ontario NOB 1T0. http://porcupinesquill.ca

Represented in Canada by the Literary Press Group.
Trade orders are available from University of Toronto Press.

We acknowledge the support of the Ontario Arts Council and the Canada
Council for the Arts for our publishing program. The financial support of
the Government of Canada through the Canada Book Fund is also gratefully
acknowledged. Thanks, also, to the Government of Ontario through the
Ontario Media Development Corporation's Ontario Book Initiative.

PS
8701
.V5
A6
2010

ONTARIO ARTS COUNCIL
CONSEIL DES ARTS DE L'ONTARIO

Canada Council   Conseil des Arts
for the Arts   du Canada

Table of Contents

Foreword

Who was the real Margaret Avison? Regarded by some as a poet's poet, credited as one of the first to bring modernism to Canadian poetry, considered by many a difficult poet, always a favourite of academics, Avison was from the beginning taken seriously – her linguistically vibrant poems admired, analyzed, and much written-about. Canada honoured her first book, *Winter Sun*, with its highest literary award. But to the discomfiture of some readers, her embrace of Christianity in 1963 brought to her work a new preoccupation. The 1960s, when Western intellectuals and artists were exploring Far Eastern spiritual traditions, was an inauspicious time to be writing faith-based Christian poetry. Some mainstream poets and critics, unable to relate to Avison's Christian poems, dismissed them as inferior to her early work, while a new readership of co-religionists embraced her as a 'Christian poet'.

Yet this, like so many statements one could make about Avison, is an oversimplification. It is not as though, from a certain point onward, Avison wrote only on Christian themes. Her poems after conversion continued to explore a range of subjects and to reflect the same compassionate humanism, attunement to nature, keenness of observation, and questioning spirit that had characterized her earlier work. Moreover, one can't so easily separate Avison's 'Christian' poems from her work at large. Scriptural allusions and poems based on Bible narratives appear in many early poems. Is 'The Butterfly', which refers to 'the Voice that stilled the sea of Galilee', a Christian poem? It was written a full two decades before her conversion experience. Are later poems like 'Hid Life' and 'Released Flow', or 'Cement Worker on a Hot Day', Christian poems? A spiritual subtext is easily discerned, yet there is nothing specifically Christian or even overtly religious in them.

Another oversimplification links Avison with certain American poets (notably Cid Corman, with whom she corresponded for years, and the Black Mountain Poets). More has been made of this association, probably, than it warrants. Avison never considered herself part of any movement. She partook of the energy, and found validation in the interest and camaraderie offered by fellow poets, but went her own way. Still, as a singular woman poet who won the respect of a group of prominent male peers, she seems a natural descendant of Marianne Moore and Elisabeth Bishop.

Avison's poems exhibit a range of forms and styles, yet in every mode a voice comes through that is uniquely recognizable as hers – a response to the world that seamlessly blends the cerebral, the sensory, and the emotive. She broaches the metaphysical and theological by way of the concrete, the physical, the social and human, delineating these with almost hallucinatory attention to detail. A wide-ranging allusiveness reflects eclectic reading, but equal attention is given to the unmediated 'real world' (primarily an urban world, rendered with haunting vividness through changes of season and times of day). The simplest poems about the weather today, or the view out the window, easily yield a metaphoric reading, yet can also satisfy as poems about the weather or the view out the window.

Most distinctive is Avison's singular diction, often inseparable from her singularity of perception. Synaesthesia ('perfumes, furs, and black-and-silver / crisscross of seasonal conversation'), new-minted compounds ('a saucepantilt of water'), words used in unexpected ways ('birds clotted in big trees') combine to create a density of effect that can seem almost baroque at one moment ('the path-dust is nutmeg powdered and/ bird-foot embroidered'), tautly economical at another ('Horsepower crops Araby for pasture'). Where but in an Avison poem do 'astonished cinders quake with rhizomes', where else will we hear named, and recognize, a faint clicking sound that might be the 'conversational side-effect / among the pigeons' – or encounter the 'uncontrollable beautiful / sheepdogging skypower' of a sudden rainstorm?

Avison herself felt that if her early poetry was difficult, this was a shortcoming: she spoke of her process as one of growing simpler. Yet her most-quoted lines come from one of her most hermetic poems, the sonnet 'Snow': 'Nobody stuffs the world in at your eyes. / The optic heart must venture: a jailbreak / and re-creation.' The rest of that poem poses a huge challenge to any would-be interpreter, and has invited some wildly different readings; but the opening lines seem to speak clearly and memorably to everyone who hears them. Other early poems that have been favourites ('The Swimmer's Moment', 'New Year's Poem', 'Thaw') share this resonant access-ibility. Yet even at their most strange, Avison's poems address the reader with a magnetic intimacy. They beguile with sharp flashes of the familiar – tableaux and moments that we recognize, even when the meaning of the whole eludes us – and their mysteriousness feels like the mysteriousness of life itself.

Particularly in the early poems there's a lot of rhyme, even where the rhythms are free. 'Snow' is one of a series of four sonnets in *Winter Sun* (in one of which, not included here, Avison expresses her ambivalence about this form). Poems in rhyming quatrains appear in all her collections, and these show a surprising range of tone (note the wit of 'Mordent for a Melody', the lyrical dreaminess of 'Thaw', the Dickinson-like 'Oughtiness Ousted', the conversational 'Safe but Shaky'). Formal considerations aside, the poems are diverse in what they do. Some, like 'All Fools' Eve', 'The World Still Needs', 'September Street', turn a panoramic, bird's-eye-view lens on the world, showing us a cross-section of life in a series of sharply detailed but distanced vignettes. By contrast, 'Pace', 'Twilight', and 'A Nameless One' magnify their closely observed particulars with an intense, slowed-down focus. There are poems that observe people in daily moments ('In a Season of Unemployment', 'Scar-face', 'Cement Worker on a Hot Day', 'Power'); poems in which unidentified, disembodied voices are heard conversing ('Pace', 'Many as Two', 'A Story'); and occasional flights into lush lyricism ('Jonathan, O Jonathan', 'July Man').

Avison's overtly Christian poems display similar diversity. They include scriptural glosses, prayers, poems about the life of Jesus, poems celebrating moments on the Christian calendar, and poems of personal moral struggle. The long poem 'A Story' represents a turning point, the first poem after conversion. A modern-day retelling of the parable of the sower and the seed (Matthew 13: 1-23), this poem in dialogue form is cunningly layered: story within story within story, a parable *about* a parable. The primary speaker tells a story about *hearing* a story, communicating both the story and the experience of hearing it to somebody else. In effect, the poem enacts the parable. Yet 'A Story' feels archetypal as much as Christian. Remarkable in the recounting is the way the storyteller in the boat and the figure of the gardener in the story blend into one mysterious, numinous, benevolent presence – prompting the second speaker's almost reluctant, wondering question: 'Where is he now?'

Avison's later work did become simpler – less virtuosic in its associative leaps, less intricate in vocabulary, more conversational in tone. While many early poems begin in philosophical statement ('Frivolity is out of season', 'The world doesn't crumble apart'), later ones are more apt to begin in a question ('Why are we / so often not / any different?') Avison's became more and more a poetry of inquiry, an inner pondering of her daily givens, to which we are made party. Her question mark is a straw to the wind, testing premises, language, commonly held beliefs or interpretations, familiar texts, the evidence of her own senses. And it's our luck that her explorations include us in their process, tugging us along until they come to rest at a stopping point that is always just that – a stopping point, nothing so final as closure.

– ROBYN SARAH

The Butterfly

An uproar,
a spruce-green sky, bound in iron,
the murky sea running a sulphur scum,
I saw a butterfly, suddenly.
It clung between the ribs of the storm, wavering,
and flung against the battering bone-wind.
I remember it, glued to the grit of that rain-strewn beach
that glowered around it, swallowed its startled design
in the larger iridescence of unstrung dark.

That wild, sour air, those miles of crouching forest, that moth
when all enveloping space
is a thin glass globe, swirling with storm
tempt us to stare, and seize analogies.
The Voice that stilled the sea of Galilee
overtoned by the new peace, the fierce subhuman peace
of such an east sky, blanched like Eternity.

The meaning of the moth, even the smashed moth, the
meaning of the moth –
can't we stab that one angle into the curve of space
that sweeps so unrelenting, far above,
towards the subhuman swamp of under-dark?

.

Snow

Nobody stuffs the world in at your eyes.
The optic heart must venture: a jail-break
And re-creation. Sedges and wild rice
Chase rivery pewter. The astonished cinders quake
With rhizomes. All ways through the electric air
Trundle candy-bright discs; they are desolate
Toys if the soul's gates seal, and cannot bear,
Must shudder under, creation's unseen freight.
But soft, there is snow's legend: colour of mourning
Along the yellow Yangtze where the wheel
Spins an indifferent stasis that's death's warning.
Asters of tumbled quietness reveal
Their petals. Suffering this starry blur
The rest may ring your change, sad listener.

Jonathan, O Jonathan

The spokes of sun
have pronged and spun:
a bowling barrow – paddle-wheel – or rein
held taut. Careening
early this morning
shod hooves flaked the loose tiles. Sky opened. Horning
farness flooded through.
The high-swivelling blue,
the wet-clay cumulus, and the rough fleur-de-lys
fringing it, ensource
an unroofed universe,
lettuce-cool largeness. The wrenched miles swing and course,
rivers of speed.
The oven-bread
of earth smokes rainbows. Blind stars and swallows parade
the windy sky of streets
and cheering beats
down faintly, to leaves in sticks, insects in pleats
and pouches hidden
and micro-garden.
At the kitchen-door of their forwardfold backslidden
munching wishes, men,
shouting and toppling
smokestacks like Saturday children, suddenly crane
for the still make-wish.
Where the roofs slope and flash
are hearts pungent and herbal for the sungold wheels to crush.

The World Still Needs

Frivolity is out of season.
Yet, in this poetry, let it be admitted
The world still needs piano-tuners
And has fewer, and more of these
Grey fellows prone to liquor
On an unlikely Tuesday, gritty with wind,
When somewhere, behind windows,
A housewife stays for him until the
      Hour of the uneasy bridge-club cocktails
      And the office rush at the groceteria
      And the vesper-bell and lit-up buses passing
      And the supper trays along the hospital corridor,
Suffering from
Sore throat and dusty curtains.

Not all alone on the deserted boathouse
Or even on the prairie freight
(The engineer leaned out, watchful and blank
And had no Christmas worries
Mainly because it was the eve of April),
Is like the moment
When the piano in the concert-hall
Finds texture absolute, a single solitude
For those hundreds in rows, half out of overcoats,
Their eyes swimming with sleep.

From this communal cramp of understanding
Springs up suburbia, where every man would build
A clapboard in a well of Russian forest
With yard enough for a high clothesline strung
To a small balcony ...
A woman whose eyes shine like evening's star
Takes in the freshblown linen
While sky a lonely wash of pink is still
Reflected in brown mud
Where lettuces will grow, another spring.

All Fools' Eve

From rooming-house to rooming-house
The toasted evening spells
City to hayrick, warming and bewildering
A million motes. From gilded tiers,
Balconies, and sombre rows,
Women see gopher-hawks, and rolling flaxen hills;
Smell a lost childhood's homely supper.
Men lean with folded newspapers,
Touched by a mushroom and root-cellar
Coolness. The wind flows,
Ruffles, unquickens. Crumbling ash
Leaves the west chill. The Sticks-&-Stones, this City,
Lies funeral bare.
Over its gaping arches stares
That haunt, the mirror mineral.
In cribs, or propped at plastic tablecloths,
Children are roundeyed, caught by a cold magic,
Fading of glory. In their dim
Cement-floored garden the zoo monkeys shiver.
Doors slam. Lights snap, restore
The night's right prose.
Gradually
All but the lovers' ghostly windows close.

Hiatus

The weedy light through the uncurtained glass
Finds foreign space where the piano was,
And mournful airs from the propped-open door
Follow forlorn shreds of excelsior.
Though the towel droops with sad significance
All else is gone; one last reviewing glance,
One last misplacing, finding of the key,
And the last steps echo, and fade, and die.
Then wanderer, with a hundred things to see to,
Scores of decisions waiting on your veto,
Or worse, being made at random till you come
So weeks will pass before you feel at home,
Mover unmoved, how can you choose this hour
To prowl at large around a hardware store?
When you have purchased the superfluous wrench
You wander still, and watch the late sun drench
The fruit-stalls, pavements, shoppers, cars, as though
All were invisible and safe but you.
But in your mind's ear now resounds the din
Of friends who've come to help you settle in,
And your thoughts fumble, as you start the car,
On whether somebody marked the barrel where the glasses are.

November 23

A childhood friend of my friend has died suddenly.
We are not old, any of us;
None of us will be young, again.
Is it respect for my friend's grief (the estranger:
     his folded napkin and his cup
     empty, wherever people
     have waited seriously together
     alone),
Or is it the persistence
Of harbour fog-horn, cars,
My neighbour muttering to herself,
Not bothering not to, when
Stillness glimmers beyond there – just beyond the senses –
That makes me sweat with vertigo
On this peculiar shelf
Of being?

New Year's Poem

The Christmas twigs crispen and needles rattle
Along the window-ledge.
       A solitary pearl
Shed from the necklace spilled at last week's party
Lies in the suety, snow-luminous plainness
Of morning, on the window-ledge beside them.
And all the furniture that circled stately
And hospitable when these rooms were brimmed
With perfumes, furs, and black-and-silver
Crisscross of seasonal conversation, lapses
Into its previous largeness.
       I remember
Anne's rose-sweet gravity, and the stiff grave
Where cold so little can contain;
I mark the queer delightful skull and crossbones
Starlings and sparrows left, taking the crust,
And the long loop of winter wind
Smoothing its arc from dark Arcturus down
To the bricked corner of the drifted courtyard,
And the still window-ledge.
       Gentle and just pleasure
It is, being human, to have won from space
This unchill, habitable interior
Which mirrors quietly the light
Of the snow, and the new year.

The Swimmer's Moment

For everyone
The swimmer's moment at the whirlpool comes,
But many at that moment will not say
'This is the whirlpool, then.'
By their refusal they are saved
From the black pit, and also from contesting
The deadly rapids and emerging in
The mysterious, and more ample, further waters.
And so their bland-blank faces turn and turn
Pale and forever on the rim of suction
They will not recognize.
Of those who dare the knowledge
Many are whirled into the ominous centre
That, gaping vertical, seals up
For them an eternal boon of privacy,
So that we turn away from their defeat
With a despair, not for their deaths, but for
Ourselves, who cannot penetrate their secret
Nor even guess at the anonymous breadth
Where one or two have won:
(The silver reaches of the estuary).

September Street

Harvest apples lack tartness.
The youngest child stares at the brick school wall.
After the surprising *coup* at a late luncheon meeting
the young man shifting for green concludes
the future makes his bitten thumb the fake.
A convalescent steps around
wet leaves, resolving on the post-box corner.
Next time, the young man glimpses,
he will be one of three, not the lone fourth
susceptible to elation.
Yellow. The pride saddens him.
A van grinds past. Somebody with
considerable dash and a strong left hand
plays 'Annie Laurie' on an untuned piano.
Granada will not rhyme with Canada.
The home-grown wines have sharpness.
A scissor-grinder used to come
about the hour the school let out
and children knocked down chestnuts.
On the yellow porch
one sits, not reading headlines; the old eyes
read far out into the mild
air, runes.
See. There: a stray sea-gull.

Watershed

The world doesn't crumble apart.
The general, and rewarding, illusion
Prevents it. You know what you know in your heart
But there is no traffic in that direction,
Only acres of stained quicksand,
       Stained by the sun
That lingers still at a Muscovite level, ignoring
The clocks in the wrists and the temples, and up in the towers
That you see as you walk, assuming the earth your floor
Though you know in your heart that the foot-hold really is gone.

(I saw you come out of the painted grove, my buck,
With the bruise of leaf-wet under your eyes,
      In a shy terrible blaze.
  The painted grove, hung stiffly with cold wax
  And fading pigments, issued you complete
And tissued then in myriad light-spots, swivelling
Into sheerest space. It was bright and spacious and neat
With everything moving, pricking from points of clear:
      Day-bourne.)

There is a change in the air:
The rain and the dark and the bare
Bunched trees, in pewter fresco, square
From the window. Yes, and you know
In your heart what chill winds blow.
And the clocks in the temples, in all the towers, sound on
(Quarter and half), and the gutters flow, and the sour
Rain pastes the leather-black streets with large pale leaves.

Thaw

Sticky inside their winter suits
The Sunday children stare at pools
In pavement and black ice where roots
Of sky in moodier sky dissolve.

An empty coach train runs along
The thin and sooty river flats
And stick and straw and random stones
Steam faintly when its steam departs.

Lime-water and liquorice light
Wander the tumbled streets. A few
Sparrows gather. A dog barks out
Under the dogless pale pale blue.

Move your tongue along a slat
Of a raspberry box from last year's crate.
Smell a saucepantilt of water
On the coal-ash in your grate.

Think how the Black Death made men dance,
And from the silt of centuries
The proof is now scraped bare that once
Troy fell and Pompey scorched and froze.

A boy alone out in the court
Whacks with his hockey-stick, and whacks
In the wet, and the pigeons flutter, and rise,
And settle back.

Mordent for a Melody

Horsepower crops Araby for pasture.
TV glides past the comet's fin.
No question, time is moving faster
And, maybe, space is curling in.

Seething with atoms, trifles show
The Milky Way in replica.
Clip but fingernail, and lo!
A supernova drops away.

Spinning ourselves at stunning speed,
Within our envelope of air
We spin again. The derricks bleed
To spark us round and round our sphere.

Things are arranged in series. What
Appears but once we never see.
Yet someone, streaking by then, caught
Crescendos of conformity,

Reported them a unit, proved
Proliferation serves its turn.
(How can the Engineer above
Refuel, at the rate we burn?)

Sleep has a secret tempo. Man
Swerves back to it, out of the glare,
And finds that each recurring dawn
Wakes Rip Van Winkles everywhere.

Dance of the midges in the warm
Sand reaches of infinity,
May this invisible music swarm
Our spirits, make them hep, and we

Sing with our busy wings a gay
Pas de million until our singeing-day.

The Typographer's Ornate Symbol
at the End of a Chapter or a Story

This is another time.
Somebody turned a leaf in a book.
A reader.
To him I am smaller than the
wrinkle on his thumb-knuckle
which also he
need never see
and nonetheless
has.
It is not pity about me for all that.

My plain daylight
is a plainness
of particular beauty.

This is another time.
The lilac lobs, not
pretty, left alone,
alive,
in the clumsy flume
of patch-bricked wind.

The same day the chestnuts lit their
fadey chandeliers
and bees put on their
shrunk wool swimming suits,
the pump-hose poured a
river of quick-setting cement over
two men in an earthwork: a
foreman; an
engineer.

The clock-face has its glass
against the whinstone
sky.
This is another time.

If the reader stirs and fetches a
sigh, turning his page,
my sigh is as the
wild barley's,
a small stir from
a cool place.
Some asking of brazen questions has
had its season.
This is not autumn,
not one of the Four.
This is another time.

The book and that
blunt reader ... the turning of a page ...
maybe the whole *bibliothèque* vanished there, a
language lost.

It is not pity about me for all that.

Pace

'Plump raindrops in these
faintly clicking groves,
the pedestrians' place, July's
violet and albumen
close?'

'No. No. It is perhaps the conversational side-effect
among the pigeons; behold
the path-dust is nutmeg powdered and
bird-foot embroidered.'

   The silk-fringed hideaway
   permits the beechnut-cracking
   squirrels to plumply
   pick and click and
   not listen.

Pedestrians linger
striped stippled sunfloating
  at the rim of the
    thin-wearing groves

letting the ear experience this
discrete, delicate
clicking.

Twilight

Three minutes ago it was almost dark.
Now all the darkness is in the
leaves (there are no more
low garage roofs, etc.).

But the sky itself has become mauve.
Yet it is raining.
The trees rustle and tap with rain.
... Yet the sun is gone.
It would even be gone from the mountaintops
if there were mountains.

In cities this mauve sky
may be of man.

The taps listen, in the unlighted bathroom.

Perfume of light.

It is gone. It is all over:
until the hills close to behind
the ultimate straggler, it will
never
be so again.

The insect of thought retracts its claws;
it wilts.

In a Season of Unemployment

These green painted park benches are
all new. The Park Commissioner had them
planted.
Sparrows go on
having dust baths at the edge of
the park maple's shadow, just where
the bench is cemented down, planted
and then cemented.

> Not a breath moves
> this newspaper.
> I'd rather read it by the Lapland sun at midnight. Here we're
> bricked in early by a
> stifling dark.

On that bench a man in a
pencil-striped white shirt
keeps his head up and steady.

> The newspaper-astronaut says
> 'I feel excellent under the condition of weightlessness.'
> And from his bench a
> scatter of black bands in the hollow-air
> ray out – too quick for the eye –
> and cease.

> 'Ground observers watching him on a TV circuit said
> At the time of this report he
> was smiling,' Moscow ra-
> dio reported.
> I glance across at him, and mark that
> he is feeling
> excellent too, I guess, and
> weightless and
> 'smiling'.

July Man

Old, rain-wrinkled, time-soiled, city-wise, morning man
whose weeping is for the dust of the elm-flowers
and the hurting motes of time,
rotted with rotting grape,
sweet with the fumes,
puzzled for good by fermented potato-
peel out of the vat of the times,
turned out and left
in this grass-patch, this city-gardener's place
under the buzzing populace's
square shadows, and the green shadows
of elm and ginkgo and lime
(planted for Sunday strollers and summer evening
families, and for those
bird-cranks with bread-crumbs
and crumpled umbrellas who come
while the dew is wet on the park, and beauty
is fan-tailed, grey and dove grey, aslant, folding in
from the white fury of day).

In the sound of the fountain
you rest, at the cinder-rim, on your bench.

The rushing river of cars
makes you a stillness, a pivot, a heart-stopping
blurt, in the sorrow
of the last rubbydub swig, the searing, and
stone-jar solitude lost, and yet,
and still – wonder (for good now) and
trembling:

> The too much none of us knows
> is weight, sudden sunlight, falling
> on your hands and arms, in your lap,
> all, all, in time.

A Nameless One

Hot in June a narrow winged
long-elbowed-thread-legged
living insect lived
and died within
the lodgers' second-floor bathroom here.

At six a.m.
wafting ceilingward,
no breeze but what it living made there;

at noon standing
still as a constellation of spruce needles
before the moment of
making it, whirling;

at four a
wilted flotsam, cornsilk, on the linoleum:

now that it is
over, I
look with new eyes
upon this room
adequate for one to
be, in.

Its insect-day
has threaded a needle
for me for my eyes dimming
over rips and tears and
thin places.

Many As Two

'Where there is the green thing
life springs clean.'
      Yes. There is blessed life, in
      bywaters; and in pondslime
      but not for your drinking.
'Where the heart's room
deepens, and the thrum
of the touched heartstrings reverberates – *Vroom* –
there I am home.'
      Yes. And the flesh's doom
      is – a finally welcome going out on a limb?
      or a terror you who love dare not name?
      (No thing abiding.)
No sign, no magic, no roadmap, no
pre-tested foothold. 'Only that you know
there is the way, plain,
and the home-going.'

Outside the heartbreak home I know, I can own
no other.
      'The brokenness. I know.
      Alone.'
(Go with us, then?)

A Story

Where *were* you then?
         At the beach.
With your crowd again.
Trailing around, open
to whatever's going. Which one's
calling for you tonight?
         Nobody.
I'm sorry I talk so. Young
is young. I ought to remember
and let you go and be glad.
         No. It's all right.
         I'd just sooner stay home.
You're not sick? did you
get too much sun? a crowd,
I never have liked it, safety in numbers
indeed!
         He was alone.
Who was alone?
         The one
         out on the water, telling
         something. He sat in the boat that
         they shoved out for him, and told
         us things. We all just stood there
         about an hour. Nobody
         shoving. I couldn't see
         very clearly, but I listened
         the same as the rest.
What was it about?
         About a giant, sort of.
         No. No baby-book giant.
         But about a man. I think –
You *are* all right?
         Of course.
Then tell me
so I can follow. You all

standing there, getting up
out of the beach-towels and gathering
out of the cars, and the ones
half-dressed, not even caring –
      Yes. Because the ones
      who started to crowd around were
      so still. You couldn't
      help wondering. And it spread.
      And then when I would have felt out of it
      he got the boat, and I could
      see the white, a little, and
      hear him, word by word.
What did he tell the lot of you
to make you stand? Politics?
Preaching? You can't believe everything
they tell you, remember –
      No. More, well a
      fable. Honestly, I –
I won't keep interrupting.
I'd really like you to tell.
Tell me. I won't say anything.
      It is a story. But
      only one man comes.
      Tall, sunburnt, coming
      not hurried, but as though
      there was so much power in reserve
      that walking all day and night
      would be lovelier than sleeping if
      sleeping meant missing it, easy
      and alive, and out there.
Where was it?
      On a kind of clamshell back.
      I mean country, like round about here,
      but his tallness, as he walked there

made green and rock-grey and brown
his floorway. And sky a brightness.
What was he doing? Just walking?
No. Now it sounds strange
but it wasn't, to hear.
He was casting seed,
only everywhere.
On the roadway, out
on the baldest stone,
on the tussocky waste
and in pockets of loam.
Seed? A farmer?
A gardener rather
but there was nothing
like garden, mother.
Only the queer
dark way he went
and the star-shine of
the seed he spent.
(Seed you could see that way –)
In showers. His fingers
shed, like the gold
of blowing autumnal
woods in the wild.
He carried no wallet
or pouch or sack,
but clouds of birds followed
to buffet and peck
on the road. And the rock
sprouted new blades
and thistle and stalk
matted in, and the birds
ran threading the tall grasses
lush and fine
in the pockets of deep earth –

You mean, in time
he left, and you saw
this happen?
      The hollow
      air scalded with sun.
      The first blades went sallow
      and dried, and the one
      who had walked, had only
      the choked-weed patches
      and a few thin files
      of windily, sunnily
      searching thirsty ones
      for his garden
      in all that place.
      But they flowered, and shed
      their strange heart's force
      in that wondering wilderness –
Where is he now?
      The gardener?
No. The storyteller
out on the water?
      He is alone.

      Perhaps a few
      who beached the boat and
      stayed, would know.

The Dumbfounding

When you walked here,
took skin, muscle, hair,
eyes, larynx, we
withheld all honour: 'His house is clay,
how can he tell us of his far country?'

Your not familiar pace
in flesh, across the waves,
woke only our distrust.
Twice-torn we cried 'A ghost'
and only on our planks counted you fast.

Dust wet with your spittle
cleared mortal trouble.
We called you a blasphemer,
a devil-tamer.

The evening you spoke of going away
we could not stay.
All legions massed. You had to wash, and rise,
alone, and face
out of the light, for us.

You died.
We said,
'The worst is true, our bliss
has come to this.'

When you were seen by men
in holy flesh again
we hoped so despairingly for such report
we closed their windpipes for it.

Now you have sought
and seek, in all our ways, all thoughts,
streets, musics – and we make of these a din
trying to lock you out, or in,
to be intent. And dying.

Yet you are
constant and sure,
the all-lovely, all-men's-way
to that far country.

Lead through the garden to
trash, rubble, hill,
where, the outcast's outcast, you
sound dark's uttermost, strangely light-brimming, until
time be full.

Oughtiness Ousted

God (being good) has let me know
no good apart from Him.
He, knowing me, yet promised too
all good in His good time.

This light, shone in, wakened a hope
that lives in here-and-now;
strongly the wind in push and sweep
made fresh for all-things-new.

But O, how very soon a gloat
gulped joy: the kernel (whole)
I chaffed to merely *act* and *ought* –
'rightness' uncordial.

But Goodness broke in, as the sea
satins in shoreward sun
washing the clutter wide away:
all my inventeds gone.

Hid Life

Red apples hang frozen
in a stick-dry, snow-dusty
network of branches,
against lamb's wool and pastelblue of sky,
a crooked woodenness, a wizening red.

Are these iron stems? or is
this tree in a lee out of the
clattering winds?

Heavily in my heart
the frost-bruised fruit, the sombre tree,
this unvisited room off winter's endless corridors
weigh down.

       But
even this fruit's flesh
will sodden down at last.

Botanist, does the seed
so long up held
still somehow inform
petal and apple-spring-perfume
for sure, from so far?

Is the weight only
a waiting?

Slow Advent

In silver candy seeds
worked into shortbreads,
a manger and
pentangle star
       – oh, how to utter?
The all-enabling Infant 'lulled'
in romance verses,
and plaster, painted, amidst stagehands'
hay and incense
       – oh, how to express
           even the animal *richesse?*
Stitched in wool
on kindergarten paper and
in electrical street-dangles, aglow,
the emblems
       – oh, I too desecrate
       the holy hush
          to trumpet:

joy in the newborn, so
far, His
coming, so
small to all my anticipating sense of
majesty, yet

indomitably coming:
the flint-set-faced
ready-for-gallows One,
on, on, into glory, and His
place of my being to be
His as will every
place
be.

Released Flow

In the sunward sugarbush
runnels shine and down-rush
through burning snow and thicket-slope.
The spiced air is ocean-deep.

Melting ridge and rivermouth
shape the waters in the earth
and the motions of the light
close the flow as watertight.

> 'In and out the windows'
> squirrels flip and play
> through sunsplash and high and low
> in winter's gallery.

The extraordinary beyond the hill
breathes   and is   imperturbable.
Near the gashed bough the hornets fur
in paperpalace-keep and -choir.

Across snowmush and sunstriped maples
honeyed woodsmoke curls and scrolls.
Sunblue and bud and shoot wait to unlatch
all lookings-forth, at the implicit touch.

Cement Worker on a Hot Day

I've passed this yellow hydrant
in sun and sleet, at dusk –
        just a knob
          shape.

Now, here, this afternoon
suddenly a man
stops work on the new curb in
the oils of sun,

            and (why of course!)
            wrenches the hydrant till
            it yields a gush
            for him to gulp and wash in.

Yes   yes   a hydrant
was always there but now
it's his,   and flows.

Scar-face

Scarred – beyond what plastic surgery
could do, or where
no surgeon was when blasted
in the wilds or
        on a side road –

he prows his life through
the street's flow and wash
of others' looks.

His face is a good
face, looking-out-from.

A Lament

A gizzard and some ruby inner parts
glisten here on the path where wind has parted
the fall field's silken ashblonde.

I fumble in our fault
('earth felt the wound,' said Milton).
Cobwebs of hair glued
to cheekbone, among
gnat eddies and silences,
I clamber on through papery leaves and slick
leathering leaves between
the stifling meadows.

Eyeblink past blue,   the far
suns herd their flocks.

Crumbling comes,
voracious, mild as loam –
but not restoring.   Death has us glassed in
for all the fine airflow and the
auburn and wickerwork beauty of this valley.

Somewhere a hawk swings, stronger,
or a weasel's eyes brighten.

The viscera still shine
with sun, by weed and silver riverflow.

Noted, Foundered

The tap of a carpenter's hammer
out on the lot.
The neighbour's tread on the tired stairs,
feeling her way, having bought
pinched loaves, waxpaper farmer's cheese, two chops,
stiffpaper sugar, wilt-paper greens, paperwet butter, and
the papers, trudging because she is hot.
These two pace the stutter and whir
of sewing-machine thought at its simple seam.

Somewhere a maiden spins in her prison in a tower.
She will endure for a hundred years but
she's licked from the start.

These are the masks of the midcontinent
where sea once moved, a seabed levelled, dried,
baked, abandoned, ours for this interim-ever.
Cities sprouted, bulged,
jostled for shine at sunset.
Rails and runways gleam and blink.

The carpenter still taps. The neighbour's aged parent
is dying in the civic hospital.

Power

Master of his first tricycle,
pedalling furiously towards the singing
lethal traffic
he – double elation – meets
his father fresh afoot from that main thoroughfare –
        to circle and
            come too? No – a palaver
in reasonable terms he mutinously
waits out, stubbed between lawn and father's foot,
all dammed-up and high voltage
with ears for where he'll go
only.
At last dad hoists him, waist under one arm
trike dangled from the other hand
and heads home.

DON'T PICK ME UP! the scarlet
struggling sobbing adventurer
wails (after the fact).

One is so powerful.
One is so small.

How can power know
not to make helplessness
what is decisive?

Loss

Back window with red-checked oilcloth on the sill
and orange-red geraniums the leaves wrinkly
in sunlight, root-cellar boards, a clothesline,
lower fence caving valleyward where the worn
grass and feathery vegetable plot give way to
butter-and-eggs, among some bluish
perennial sweet peas:
the place is bared. Trees are long gone,
and the clutter of children gone
and the sun washes in to the bone.

Here pain hit home.

Its home makes the plain place
invisibly surge with beauty, almost unbearable
while it is day.

Crowd Corralling

Hard rain.
the bean-mash smell.
leaky tin-brim spill.
grass-soak:

birds clotted in big trees.
Cotton people in go-holes:

uncontrollable beautiful
sheepdogging skypower!

Lit Sky and Foundered Earth

The nighthawk? no, a gull
far off, only affirms
the quiet of this hour,
as do the children's cries
in the near-dark – still playing,
guilty with freedom, after
this sudden summer on a
school day in October:
Hearing them, you know how
flushed their faces, how
desperate for one last dare:
they listen too for that
voice from a lit window or doorway
to beam them down, and in.

Poring

These words*become
opaque when wrestled down.
They're plain but ponderous
with pastness.

Yet there begins to
emerge – see! – far,
farther: a distinct design,
like miniature landscapes in the sun
out through the arch in a Gozzoli
painting.

Out of the numbing
pastness opens an – escape!
an invitation? One expects
to breathe that light
somehow, and perhaps see
even the grassblades, and the
shadows of the grassblades.

---

*E.g., in Leviticus

Balancing Out

He smells of – what?
It's like wet coal-dust.
He came very late:
tangled brown hair, his face
streaked, and bleary;
no gloves, but (Merry
Christmas) from a mission, twice
blest – a good warm coat
that could go anywhere – and had!
now puckered, snagged, hem spread
from sleeping out, and ripped
around one leather elbow.
and buttoned crooked. There were no
other buttons now. He slept
there in his pew.

The giver of his topcoat eerily
watched, her widow's desolation clearly
inconsolable now
(a pang – like joy!),
to see what she had seen
on a fine and steady man
made come full circle on this ruined fellow.

Still, he had his coat,
and she, the echoing years.

Sad Song

You open your eyes on a lonely light.
Something not there you'd dreamed would be.
Utterly lost from all company you
yield to an absence from long ago
looking for pencil-tracings out on the
waiting wash of the lonely light.

Finished When Unfinished

On a flat stone, in the
plain light, lies a
torn paper with something written
on it. All the wide shore, the
calm lake, the reeds
listen in the sun, in
silence, as do other flat stones.

Writing to read? for a bird in
transit, or for the
breeze that sometimes stirs when a
motionless midday
passes? No one
is left, writer or some
incurious wanderer now
long gone.
      Here is only
peacefulness, and several sunny
flat stones.

Prayer of Anticipation

Jesus, interpreter – more,
configurer of all
that has deepened
odd moments for me from
the outset, you are as if
strolling through the
morning, saying those
fierce, or disarming, words
within the word.

If you approach through
a clutter, nothing need
hinder you, who gave
the deaf hearing, and not
waiting always to be
besought, for the
initiative is yours, is the
essential.

It is my best good
to let you speak your
remembered, translated,
printed, painfully
accessible word.

Jesus, disclose
your journeying for
this day's avenues.

En Route

Situation: a summer fisherman
had packed away his gear
towards homegoing, but rocked
in the quiet inlet water,
hearing it, hearing
the breezes sift across
Georgian Bay's massive
shore of rock, hearing
the lightsome heartbeat of peace.

The breeze was stiffening.
He hauled aboard
the roped anchor, clumsily
poled away the cliff of shore,
readied both oars, and set out.
In the broad bay the only
rocks to steer clear of
were near that one large island.

The dip and slap had become
bumps out there
on open water ...

Then what? *Then* what?

The future lay
ahead of him, as of us.
Rising winds can be threatening
here too, for any who
left it too late to
remember to
head homeward. People are
potential crises, scattered everywhere:

on islands, isolated, bobbing about
in small craft far too far
from rescue, at home and
safe, but far too
long waiting. All
travellers sometimes feeling
they wait too long
for homegoing.

Poetry Is

Poetry is always in
unfamiliar territory.

At a ballgame when
the hit most matters
and the crowd is half-standing
already hoarse, then poetry's
eye is astray to a
quiet area to find out
who picks up the bat the runner
flung out of his runway.

Little stuff like that
poetry tucks away in
the little basket of other
scraps. There's the

cradling undergrowth in
the scrub beside a
wild raspberry bush where
a bear lay feet up feeding
but still three rubied berries
glow in the green.
He had had enough.

Then there's the way
a child's watering can
forgotten in the garden
no faucet, but the far
sky has filled. When sun
shines again it has
become a dragonfly's pretend
skating rink.

Scraps. Who carries the basket?
What will the scraps be used for?
Poetry does not care
what things are for but is
willing to listen to
any, if not everyone's,
questions.

It can happen that poetry
basket and all *is*
the unfamiliar territory
that poetry is in.

Still Life

The last two daffodils
are dying on my table.
What were once petals grope
for water, can no longer
sip, though they stand in water,
must grope the air for more.
They have transmuted from
flower to scrawny
fingers, an old woman's in
raggedy silk gloves.

The only future for
a dying flower is
compost-mash: its lingering
memorial, when the first
eggshell dawn
lifts up a new
horizon, all
in stemless daffodils,
flowering.

Metamorphosis

Why are we so
often not
any different? Oh there are
changes nobody tried to
make happen but on a
workaday level, never from
silence's special
place where it's as if
periwinkle faces play at
being zenith:
                    up, up so
mirror-silent the
glassy dimness shows the
one far flower, here, or
almost blindingly
aloft, as well.

Safe but Shaky

I know I'm safe, but scared
for fear my fingers slip
or shakiness and dread
might make me lose my grip.

I play the misanthrope
in my own pantomime.
All's well, if I will cope
a minute at a time.

The Lord, who overheard
our thoughts, and understood
how all ways disappeared
when viewed too far ahead,

decided to provide
a (print) topography,
clues to the likely road
for us to choose if we

resolve to stay the course.
Doggedly pressing on,
it may go hard, or worse,
tangle in second-guessing.

Did You too face what seemed
options? We try to practise
steadiness. Round the bend
stray dazzles still distract us.

How do You guide us back?
In any case, we're sure
You've yielded us the slack
till, jerked, we know You're there.

Is Yours that western sky
aglow? Here shadows narrow
tonight along the way.
We'll rest now, till tomorrow.

Editor's Notes

1. There are close to 450 poems in Margaret Avison's collected poems, *Always Now*; an additional 90 in *Momentary Dark* and the posthumously published *Listening*. From such abundance, I could choose only 49 pages to represent a many-faceted poet who lived to nearly ninety. This ruled out the longer poems (excepting 'A Story', which, as the first post-conversion poem, did seem 'essential'.) Biblical glosses are not represented, but 'Poring' attests to an activity important to Avison throughout her life. Avison expressed a wish that any future 'Selected' include poems from her last years. I have sought a balance between oft-anthologized favourites and some poems much less familiar, and have tried to give fair representation to the Christian-themed poems and the later poems – always looking for unity in variety, for poems that seemed to shed light on one another.

2. My selection is arranged chronologically according to the books in which poems first appeared. Two poems in From Elsewhere, a section of uncollected poems in *Always Now*, are placed according to their dates of first publication: 'The Butterfly' in A.J.M. Smith's *The Book of Canadian Poetry* (Chicago, 1943) and 'The Typographer's Ornate Symbol at the End of a Chapter or a Story' in *Origin*, January 1962.

I am deeply indebted to Joan Eichner, who in months of regular e-mail exchanges answered endless questions, offered opinions when asked, and enhanced my understanding of many poems, providing a sympathetic sounding-board as I worked through the process of selection.

About Margaret Avison

During her last years Margaret Avison wrote an autobiography, published posthumously under the title *I Am Here and Not Not-There*. It portrays a woman who indeed knew where she was, and could affirm it without reference to where she wasn't. The formulation came to Avison during a panel discussion at the Vancouver Poetry Conference in 1963. It remained her artistic credo, but on the evidence of the autobiography, was not limited to that. A calm consciousness of her own position seems to have prevailed in all areas of her life, along with an acceptance of where others were.

Avison was born in 1918 in Galt, Ontario, third and youngest child of Mabel (Kirkland) and H. Wilson Avison, a Methodist minister. The family moved to Regina in 1920 and to Calgary in 1924 before settling in Toronto when Margaret was eleven. She recalls a happy childhood: her mother played piano, her father sang; there were summer trips to Banff and further west. Margaret's maternal grandfather, joining the household after his wife died, regaled her with family tales and brought Bible stories to life for her.

The move to Toronto coincided with the crash of 1929. Though the Avisons had security and status, the Depression made itself felt. During high school, Margaret studied piano and joined the poetry club of a well-loved teacher who famously advised her to eschew the first person singular in her poems for ten years. A three-month hospitalization for anorexia nervosa, on a thirty-bed ward of the old Toronto General, awakened in her a lifelong compassion for the poor and passion for social justice. In 1936 she entered the University of Toronto's Victoria College and took a B.A. in English, then worked, through the war years and after, as a file clerk, proofreader, librarian, research assistant, freelance writer and editor. Early on, she had begun submitting poems to *The Canadian Forum*, and A.J.M. Smith included her in his 1943 Canadian poetry anthology.

Avison consciously eschewed a career: short-term or part-time contracts gave her more freedom to pursue her own writing. Commissions included a seventh-grade textbook (*History of Ontario*, 1951), a ghostwritten autobiography of Dr. A.I. Wolinsky (*A Doctor's Memoirs*, 1960) and co-translations of Hungarian poetry and prose with Ilona Duczynska (*The Plough and the Pen*, 1963, and *Acta*

Sanctorum and other tales by Josef Lengyel, 1966). She never married; the autobiography alludes briefly to a romantic disappointment, but her deeper regret was not having children. From 1955 to 1956 she worked as nursemaid for a couple with four children, grateful for this window on family life. In 1956–57, a Guggenheim Foundation grant allowed Avison to spend eight months in Chicago working on her poetry. She returned with the manuscript of *Winter Sun*, but had no luck finding a publisher until 1960, when a former employer with connections in England placed it there for her. In Canada, the book was acclaimed with a Governor General's Award.

The year 1963 was momentous for Avison. Early in January came the mystical experience that reconnected her with Christianity. While the Bible had always nourished her, she had drifted from churchgoing and fallen into the skepticism of fellow intellectuals. Initial fears that her new-found faith would displace poetry proved unfounded. In August, the Vancouver Poetry Conference brought her together with American poets Robert Creeley, Allen Ginsberg, Robert Duncan, Charles Olson and Denise Levertov (who later, as poetry editor at Norton, asked her for the manuscript of *The Dumbfounding*.) The conference was still in session when news came of her father's death. Soon after, her mother moved in with her, an arrangement lasting until Mabel Avison's death in 1985.

Avison's later years included graduate studies, two years' teaching at Scarborough College, five years of social work at a Presbyterian storefront mission, eight months as writer-in-residence at the University of Western Ontario, five years with the CBC Radio Archives, and eight more as secretary for the Mustard Seed Mission before she retired. Her poetry remained a private but compelling interest. On the urging of longtime friend Joan Eichner, who became a valued editorial assistant, *sunblue* was published in 1978. Five collections followed, two of them subsequent to the *Collected Poems*. *No Time* won Avison a second Governor General's Award, and *Concrete and Wild Carrot*, the more lavish Griffin Prize. Her involuntary words on accepting it ('This is ridiculous!') sum up how incongruous she found worldly success for the art she had pursued with quiet dedication amid other interests and activities.

Named an Officer of the Order of Canada in 1985, Margaret Avison died in 2007 at the age of eighty-nine.

– R S

Margaret Avison: A Bibliography

POETRY

Winter Sun (1960)
The Dumbfounding (1966)
sunblue (1978)
Winter Sun / The Dumbfounding: Poems 1940–66 (1982)
No Time (1989)
Selected Poems (1991)
Not Yet But Still (1997)
Concrete and Wild Carrot (2002)
Always Now: The Collected Poems (3 volumes, 2003, 2004, 2005)
Momentary Dark (2006)
Listening: Last Poems (2009)

IN TRANSLATION

Il cuore che vede (Ravenna, 2002)
    Italian translation of selected poems

Weatherings/Verwitterungen (Berlin, 2007)
    German translation of selected poems

Cemento e carota selvatica (Rome, 2008)
    Italian translation of *Concrete and Wild Carrot*

OTHER

A Kind of Perseverance (1994), 1993 Pascal Lectures, University of Waterloo

I Am Here and Not Not-There (2009), autobiography

A Kind of Perseverance (2010), reissue, with editorial additions